NORTHWEST FOREST PLAN
THE FIRST 10 YEARS (1994–2003)

Socioeconomic Monitoring Results
Volume V: Public Values and Forest Management

Susan Charnley and Ellen M. Donoghue

General Technical Report
PNW-GTR-649 Vol. V
April 2006

 United States
Department of
Agriculture

 Forest
Service

 Pacific Northwest
Research Station

Authors

Susan Charnley and **Ellen M. Donoghue** are research social scientists, U.S. Department of Agriculture, Forest Service, Pacific Northwest Research Station, P.O. Box 3890, Portland, OR 97208.

Socioeconomic Monitoring Results Volume V: Public Values and Forest Management

Susan Charnley and Ellen M. Donoghue

Northwest Forest Plan—The First 10 Years (1994–2003): Socioeconomic Monitoring Results

Susan Charnley, Technical Coordinator

U.S. Department of Agriculture, Forest Service
Pacific Northwest Research Station
Portland, Oregon
General Technical Report PNW-GTR-649 Vol. V
April 2006

Abstract

Charnley, Susan; Donoghue, Ellen M. 2006. Socioeconomic monitoring results. Volume V: public values and forest management. In: Charnley, S., tech. coord. Northwest Forest Plan—the first 10 years (1994–2003): socioeconomic monitoring results. Gen. Tech. Rep. PNW-GTR-649. Portland, OR: U.S. Department of Agriculture, Forest Service, Pacific Northwest Research Station. 23 p.

One of the Northwest Forest Plan's socioeconomic goals was to protect the forest values and environmental qualities associated with late-successional, old-growth, and aquatic ecosystems. In Volume V we address the topic of forest protection from the socioeconomic perspective. A literature review revealed that between 1990 and 2002 there has been surprisingly little change in Pacific Northwest residents' views of how Pacific Northwest forests should be managed. Throughout this period, research findings indicate that people support forest management to provide a broad set of multiple uses and both economic and environmental benefits. Nevertheless, there has consistently been a proenvironment leaning, with the majority favoring environmental over economic management objectives when asked to make a choice between them. Throughout the study period, the belief that active forest management improves forest health has predominated. However, clearcutting has consistently been unpopular, and the majority have favored old-growth protection. New forestry techniques that are not intensive are more socially acceptable.

The monitoring team also conducted interviews with community members and agency employees from four case-study areas to document their perceptions of how well the Plan has protected forest values and environmental qualities associated with late-successional, old-growth, and aquatic ecosystems on federal forest lands. The team also documented interviewees' issues and concerns relating to federal forest management. The most positive Plan effects were believed to be associated with the protection of aquatic ecosystems. Most interviewees did not distinguish Plan effects on older forests from those on forest ecosystems more generally. Although the Plan brought an end to earlier forest management practices that many considered ecologically destructive, most people interviewed did not believe federal forests were currently healthy. They believed silvicultural activity was necessary for keeping forests healthy and that not enough had occurred during the first decade of the Plan. This led to concerns about fire, insects, and disease and frustration that needed forest work was not creating local jobs. Timber harvest, forest health, and jobs were among the biggest issues of concern to community interviewees. Although interviewees overwhelmingly believed that the Plan had emphasized forest protection over community well-being, their comments reflect a perception that healthy forest ecosystems and healthy community economies can and should be linked and that those links are currently weak.

Keywords: Northwest Forest Plan, socioeconomic monitoring, forest management values, management issues and concerns.

Preface

This report is one of a set of reports produced on this 10-year anniversary of the Northwest Forest Plan (the Plan). The collection of reports attempts to answer questions about the effectiveness of the Plan based on new monitoring and research results. The set includes a series of status and trends reports, a synthesis of all regional monitoring and research results, a report on interagency information management, and a summary report.

The status and trends reports focus on establishing baselines of information from 1994, when the Plan was approved, and reporting change over the 10-year period. The status and trends series includes reports on late-successional and old-growth forests, northern spotted owl population and habitat, marbled murrelet population and habitat, watershed condition, government-to-government tribal relationships, socioeconomic conditions, and monitoring of project implementation under Plan standards and guidelines.

The synthesis report addresses questions about the effectiveness of the Plan by using the status and trends results and new research. It focuses on the validity of the Plan assumptions, differences between expectations and what actually happened, the certainty of these findings, and, finally, considerations for the future. The synthesis report is organized in two parts: Part I—introduction, context, synthesis, and summary—and Part II—socioeconomic implications, older forests, species conservation, the aquatic conservation strategy, and adaptive management and monitoring.

The report on interagency information management identifies issues and recommends solutions for resolving data and mapping problems encountered during the preparation of the set of monitoring reports. Information issues inevitably surface during analyses that require data from multiple agencies covering large geographic areas. The goal of that report is to improve the integration and acquisition of interagency data for the next comprehensive report.

The socioeconomic status and trends report is published in six volumes. Volume I of the report contains key findings. Volume II addresses the evaluation question, Are predictable levels of timber and nontimber resources available and being produced? The focus of Volume III is the evaluation question, Are local communities and economies experiencing positive or negative changes that may be associated with federal forest management? Volume IV assesses the Plan goal of promoting agency-citizen collaboration in forest management. Volume V (this volume) reports on public values regarding federal forest management in the Pacific Northwest. Volume VI provides a history of the Northwest Forest Plan socioeconomic monitoring program and a discussion of potential directions for the program.

Summary

One goal of the Northwest Forest Plan (the Plan) was to protect the forest values and environmental qualities associated with late-successional, old-growth, and aquatic ecosystems. In Volume V we address the topic of forest protection from the socioeconomic perspective. First, we report the results of a literature review that evaluates trends in public values regarding forest management in the Pacific Northwest between the early 1990s and the early 2000s. Second, we summarize the results of interviews with community members and agency employees that document their perceptions of how well the Plan has protected forest values and environmental qualities associated with late-successional, old-growth, and aquatic ecosystems on federal forest lands. We also discuss community members' issues and concerns relating to forest management under the Plan.

The monitoring questions and indicators monitored were the following:

Monitoring questions	Indicators monitored
What forest values and environmental qualities associated with federal forests are important to members of the public, and what is the balance of values (both commodity and noncommodity) that members of the public believe federal forests should be managed for?	Pacific Northwest residents' values, attitudes, and beliefs about forest management, based on a review of existing literature.
How have public attitudes, beliefs, and values relating to forest management in the Pacific Northwest changed since 1990?	
From the public perspective, how well has federal forest management under the Plan provided for forest values and environmental qualities associated with late-successional, old-growth, and aquatic ecosystems?	Community members' perceptions of of how well forest management under the Plan has achieved the goal of forest protection and provided for the forest uses, values, and environmental qualities they care about.
What issues and concerns related to federal forest management under the Plan are prevalent in local communities?	Community member's issues and concerns relating to federal forest management.

Plan Expectations Regarding Public Values

The Plan would protect the long-term health of forests, wildlife, and waterways while providing for the sustainable use of timber and nontimber forest resources.

A system of terrestrial and aquatic reserves established by the Plan would protect late-successional and old-growth forest ecosystems inside of late-successional reserves, and the health of aquatic systems and the species that depend on them in riparian reserves and key watersheds. Late-successional reserves together with other Plan land use allocations and standards and guidelines would maintain a functional older forest ecosystem. Riparian reserves would help maintain and restore riparian structures and functions, benefit fish and nonfish species dependent on riparian ecosystems, and contribute to habitat conservation for terrestrial organisms.

Monitoring Results

Between 1990 and 2002 there has been surprisingly little change in Pacific Northwest residents' views of how Pacific Northwest forests should be managed. Throughout this period, research findings indicate that people support forest management to provide a broad set of multiple uses and both economic and environmental benefits. Nevertheless, there has consistently been a pro-environment leaning, with the majority favoring environmental over economic management objectives when asked to make a choice between them. Continued support for timber production from federal forests has likely been tied to a belief that the wood products industry is important to the regional economy, and to concern for the health of rural communities. Whereas place of residence was not found to be a significant factor influencing people's attitudes, beliefs, and values about forest management prior to the Northwest Forest Plan, recent studies find that urban residents tend to be pro-environment, with rural residents having more evenly split views on forest management issues.

Throughout the study period, the belief that active forest management improves forest health has predominated. However, clearcutting has consistently been unpopular, and the majority have favored old-growth protection. New forestry techniques that are not intensive are more socially acceptable.

Have federal land managers been doing a good job of protecting the forest values and environmental qualities people care about under the Plan? The literature reviewed here does not provide extensive evidence for answering this question. The evidence that does exist suggests that opinion is fairly evenly divided. Some people have favorable views of the job forest managers are doing, and others believe that forest managers need to improve their performance.

In the four case-study locations in the Plan area where we conducted fieldwork, members of the public who were interviewed perceived that the Plan had had mixed results to date for forest protection. Their issues of concern relating to forest management were to some degree linked to those perceptions.

The most positive Plan effects were believed to be associated with the protection of aquatic ecosystems. Most interviewees did not distinguish Plan effects on older forests from those on forest ecosystems more generally. Although the Plan brought an end to earlier forest management practices that many considered ecologically destructive, most people interviewed did not believe federal forests were currently healthy. Like many Pacific Northwest residents surveyed in other studies, they believed silvicultural activity was necessary for keeping forests healthy and that not enough had occurred during the first decade of the Plan. This led to concerns about fire, insects, and disease and to frustration that needed forest work was not creating local jobs. Timber harvest, forest health, and jobs were among the biggest issues of concern to community interviewees. The others were recreation and forest access, also tied to the issue of jobs. Although interviewees overwhelmingly believed that the Plan had emphasized forest protection over community well-being, their comments reflect a perception that healthy forest ecosystems and healthy community economies can and should be linked, and that those links are currently weak.

Contents

Chapter 1: Trends in Public Attitudes, Beliefs, and Values About Forest Management in the Pacific Northwest

Susan Charnley

Introduction

The Northwest Forest Plan (the Plan) codified a shift in forest management away from the intensive timber management practices of the 1970s and 1980s toward ecosystem management. In doing so, it aimed to balance the need for forest protection with the need to provide for the sustainable use of timber and nontimber forest resources. Hence, one of the Plan's socioeconomic goals was to protect the forest values and environmental qualities associated with late-successional, old-growth, and aquatic ecosystems. These forest values include amenity values (such as scenic quality, lifestyle), environmental quality values (such as clean air and water), ecological values (such as sustainability, biodiversity), public use values (recreation), and spiritual and religious values (Donoghue 2003: 334, Stankey and Clark 1992).

The strategy used to achieve this goal was to create a reserve system on federal forest lands where the management emphasis would be on protecting late-successional and old-growth forest (older forests), endangered species, and other noncommodity values associated with the forest (Clark et al. 1999: 15). Although commodities might be produced from the reserves, they would be by-products of forest management intended to achieve ecosystem health objectives. Late-successional reserves were designed to maintain older forest ecosystems and natural ecosystem processes and to protect them from loss resulting from large-scale fire, insects and diseases, and major human impacts (USDA and USDI 1994b: B4–B5). Riparian reserves were meant to protect the health of aquatic ecosystems and the species that depend on them and to provide habitat connectivity for the late-successional reserve system (USDA and USDI 1994b: B12–B13). These two reserve types make up roughly 41 percent of the Plan area (USDA and USDI 1994b: 6–7). Another 30 percent is designated as congressionally reserved areas (such as wilderness areas or wild and scenic rivers) that mainly support noncommodity values (USDA and USDI 1994b: 6).

Other Plan monitoring is designed to collect and analyze biophysical data that will be used to assess how well the Plan has achieved the goals and expectations associated with protecting older forest habitat, associated species (northern spotted owls [*Strix occidentalis caurina*] and marbled murrelets [*Brachyramphus marmoratus*]), and aquatic and riparian ecosystems. The socioeconomic monitoring team addressed the topic of forest protection from the social perspective.

Protecting forest values and environmental qualities associated with older forests and aquatic ecosystems is a social value. Changing societal values can trigger the adaptive management process (USDA and USDI 1994a Vol. II: E4). It is important to monitor how public attitudes, beliefs, and values relating to forest management change over time so that managers can be responsive. Chapter 1 of this volume evaluates trends in public values regarding forest management in the Pacific Northwest between the early 1990s and the early 2000s.

Monitoring Questions

1. What forest values and environmental qualities associated with federal forests are important to members of the public, and what is the balance of values (both commodity and noncommodity) that members of the public believe federal forests should be managed for?
2. How have public attitudes, beliefs, and values relating to forest management in the Pacific Northwest changed since 1990?

Expectations

The Plan would protect the long-term health of forests, wildlife, and waterways while providing for the sustainable use of timber and nontimber forest resources (USDA and USDI 1994b: 2–3).

Methods

Collecting primary data on changing social values relating to federal forest management in the Plan area over time at the regional scale was beyond the scope of this monitoring program. I relied, therefore, on secondary sources documenting public views of forest management in the Pacific Northwest between 1990 and 2002 to characterize these trends. I synthesize this literature here, grouping the study findings into three periods: research conducted in 1990–94, 1995–98, and 1999–2002. The publication date of the source cited was used only when the date of research was not reported. This grouping allows comparing changing public values before and since the Plan was adopted.

Results

1990–94

A 1991 survey of 872 randomly selected Oregon residents elicited their attitudes about federal forest management by testing whether they agreed or disagreed with several different statements about forest management (Steel et al. 1994). The scale used contained five response categories that ranged from 1 (strongly disagree) to 5 (strongly agree). Respondents slightly disagreed that forests should be used primarily for timber and wood products (2.23), that more trees should be harvested to meet the needs of a larger human population (2.14), and that the primary use of forests should be to obtain products useful to people (2.53). They agreed that forest resources can be improved through silvicultural practices (4.23), that forest plants, animals, and people have an equal right to exist and develop (3.68), and that people should have more love, respect, and admiration for forests (4.04). The authors concluded that Oregonians have more "biocentric" values toward forests (values that are nature-centered) than anthropocentric values (values that are human-centered). They view forests as having a right to exist for their own sake, independent of their utility to people. They also view the noneconomic benefits from forests as deserving respect and protection, even if managing for them conflicts with economic benefits. Biocentric values contrast with "anthropocentric" values, which hold that the goal of natural resource management should be to

produce goods and services that are beneficial to people. The study found that urban and rural residents surveyed exhibited little difference in their value orientation (Steel et al. 1994). However, Oregon respondents who depended on the timber industry for their livelihood were much more likely to have anthropocentric value orientations than those who did not. And, members of environmental organizations surveyed were much more likely to have biocentric values.

The same 1991 survey found strong support for managing federal forests to support a wide range of benefits (81 percent), rather than timber and wood products alone (Shindler et al. 1993). Respondents felt that noncommodity values should be incorporated into forest management policy more strongly than they had been to date. Managing forests holistically by using an ecosystem management approach, rather than focusing on single-species management, was strongly supported (84 percent agreed). Most respondents favored balancing environmental and economic considerations in forest management decisionmaking. Only 20 percent of the respondents supported mineral exploration and extraction on federal forest lands. Roughly one-third of respondents felt that forest management should emphasize timber production (32 percent), that endangered species laws should be set aside to preserve timber jobs (37 percent), and that the survival of timber families was more important than preserving old growth (36 percent). Between 39 and 48 percent of respondents disagreed with these statements (the remainder were neutral). Oregonians surveyed were essentially divided on whether the economic vitality of local communities should be given priority when federal forest management decisions were made (46 percent agreed, 44 percent disagreed).

Finally, more than half of the respondents believed that clearcutting should be banned on federal forest lands (57 percent), that fish and wildlife habitat deserved greater protection (55 percent), and that more effort should be made to protect old growth (51 percent). (In contrast, 30 percent, 25 percent, and 32 percent of respondents disagreed with these statements, respectively). Although strong support was expressed for managing forests for multiple uses, survey respondents exhibited more of an "ecosystem-based" orientation than a "commodity-based" orientation (Shindler et al. 1993).

Proctor (1998) analyzed public comments solicited on Option 9 of the Northwest Forest Plan Draft Supplemental Environmental Impact Statement (the preferred alternative, subsequently adopted in the Plan's record of decision [USDA and USDI 1994b]). These comments came from people residing in every state in the United States and 35 foreign countries. Proctor found that an overwhelming majority of the 103,000 comments received were sympathetic to the position of environmental groups and supported the protection of old-growth forests in the Pacific Northwest. Of those people who commented specifically on Option 9, 89 percent wanted more environmental protection than Option 9 offered, expressing concerns about the effects of timber harvest on old-growth habitat. These people generally felt that the national public and future generations were more important stakeholders than local timber communities when it came to making forest management decisions. The 5 percent of commentators who wanted less protection than Option 9 provided expressed economic concerns related to its impacts on timber industry jobs. Almost all of these people lived in the Pacific Northwest region. Interestingly, all comments received—whether from pro-environmental protection or protimber interests—expressed their concerns in terms of what sets of human needs and desires associated with Pacific Northwest forests they cared about, rather than in terms of their concerns for the forests themselves. In other words, biocentric arguments supporting the intrinsic value of forests rarely surfaced. Instead, the debate focused on whether increased protection of Pacific Northwest forests would support or undermine those human needs and desires that captured their greatest interest (Proctor 1998).

Fortmann and Kusel (1990) surveyed the environmental attitudes of people living around the Klamath National Forest in northern California (one of the case-study forests in this monitoring report). A random sample of 190 members of the general public residing within 20 miles of the forest found that 28 percent had "pro-environmental" attitudes, believing land should be preserved in a natural state, and commodity uses of forests such as timber and grazing should be limited or prevented. Twenty percent of the respondents had "procommodity" attitudes, supporting commodity uses of forests. The remaining 52 percent were neutral (Fortmann and Kusel 1990: 218). These authors found no significant difference between the environmental attitudes of new rural residents from urban areas and long-time rural residents.

Summary—
Published studies that examined the environmental attitudes, beliefs, and values of Pacific Northwest residents before the Plan was adopted (1990–94) show strong support for a balanced approach to federal forest management that would incorporate a range of multiple uses, and both economic and environmental forest values. Nevertheless, a definite leaning toward the environmental and biocentric side of the scale was reported. Residential status (urban vs. rural) was not significant as an indicator of forest management views. Although not representing a random or solely local sample of Pacific Northwest residents, support for protecting old-growth forests under the Plan was overwhelming. The idea that forest health can be improved through silvicultural practices was generally supported. Most people did not support clearcutting, however.

1995–98

Between 1995 and 1997, Ribe (2002) sampled 1,035 people who were members of organized groups in western Washington and Oregon to elicit their views on the owl controversy. These organizations were of three types: those favoring forest preservation (350 members surveyed), those favoring commodity production on public land (357 members surveyed), and those with more moderate views of environmental issues (328 members surveyed). Ribe found that a majority acknowledged that there was a threat to the owl (56 percent versus 32 percent), and that there was a need to reduce timber harvest on public lands below 1980s levels to protect the owl (66 percent versus 21 percent). Respondents were divided in their views of whether the owl should be saved at a high economic cost, however (44 percent disagreed, 38 percent agreed). Clearcutting was unpopular as a harvest method across groups. Although people broadly agreed that clearcutting should be regulated (about 86 percent), no consensus was found about whether it should be banned (about 38 percent said yes, and 47 percent said no). Finally, "new forestry" techniques—those that include green-tree and down-wood retention, and selective harvesting—were found to have great potential to be socially acceptable, stable, forest management policies in the Pacific Northwest (Ribe 2002).

A survey of 1,545 randomly selected urban and rural residents living around the Gifford Pinchot National Forest in southwest Washington, and 343 other forest visitors and citizens with an interest in the forest, focused on the social acceptability of clearcutting as a forest management practice (Hansis 1995). This study found that roughly 30 percent of the respondents did not believe that clearcutting should be banned on federal forest land; roughly 56 percent did believe that clearcutting should be banned on federal forest land; and the remainder were neutral. People living in rural Washington were the most supportive of clearcutting (36 percent for, 46 percent against); interested members of the public and Portland metro-area residents were the least supportive of clearcutting on federal forest lands (26 percent for, 63 percent against).

Davis et al. (2001b) reported on the results of a statewide survey of 608 randomly chosen members of the Oregon public undertaken on behalf of the Oregon Forest Resources Institute in 1997. This survey found that most Oregonians surveyed think that forest managers need to do a better job of protecting wildlife habitat (80 percent) and fish habitat (especially for salmon) (87 percent), biodiversity (65 percent), and water quality (88 percent); and that they should do more to prevent soil erosion (88 percent). Forty-one percent of respondents thought that federal forest lands were being managed sustainably, and 39 percent did not. Although most people surveyed believed that forest managers should do a better job of providing enough timber harvest to sustain jobs in the wood products industry (63 percent), widespread concern was expressed that existing timber harvest practices were not sustainable (87 percent), and a general belief (89 percent) that finding a compromise between allowing adequate timber harvest and protecting Oregon's forests was impossible.

Summary—

The results of surveys within a few years of adopting the Plan showed that Pacific Northwest residents supported both forest protection and forest management to produce economic benefits. Strong feelings were expressed about how forests should be managed to produce those economic benefits. Most people surveyed did not support clearcutting, although support for this practice was stronger among rural residents than among urban residents. Widespread agreement was expressed that clearcutting should be regulated, but there was no broad agreement on whether it should be banned on federal forest lands. In contrast, "new forestry" techniques were found to be more socially acceptable. Finally, the vast majority of people surveyed believed that forest managers needed to do more to protect the environmental values and qualities associated with Pacific Northwest forests.

1999–2002

The Oregon Board of Forestry sponsored a study of Oregonians' attitudes, beliefs, and values about forest management on public and private forest lands in Oregon (Davis et al. 2001a, 2001b). The study, which took place in 2001, included a review of the academic literature and public opinion research on this topic, focus groups, and a telephone survey of Oregon residents. The telephone survey included 1,401 Oregonians chosen from a stratified sample based on place of residence (Davis et al. 2001a). Forest management ranked fifth on a list of 10 environmental issues of concern presented to respondents. The top environmental issue of concern was protecting water quality (scoring 4.5).[1] The three forest management goals deemed most important by survey respondents were protecting soil and water quality; maintaining the amount of forest land and ensuring harvest rates don't exceed growth rates; and protecting forests from fire, insects, disease, and invasives. When asked to weigh three different federal forest management objectives, respondents were fairly balanced in what they favored—producing forest products for human use (29 percent), protecting water

---

[1] 1 = not at all concerned, 5 = very concerned.

quality and wildlife habitat (39 percent), and meeting a wide range of social needs (32 percent). They also believed that achieving a balance between economic, environmental, recreational, and aesthetic values was possible.

Loss of forest land to development and other uses was a local issue of key concern among respondents (75 percent were very or somewhat concerned). The relation between the forest products industry and environmental groups was also a top issue of concern in local areas (scoring 4.0, with 76 percent of respondents very or somewhat concerned). The most serious issue in Oregon's rural communities was a lack of family-wage jobs (scoring 4.1),[2] followed by a perceived desire on the part of other Americans to shut down natural resource-based economies (3.9) (Davis et al. 2001a). Residents were almost evenly split on their views about whether federal forest lands were being managed sustainably to provide for the environmental, social, and economic needs of society (41 percent said yes, 39 percent said no).

Some of the relevant findings from the literature survey conducted by Davis et al. (2001b) follow.

- Whereas in 1986, 70 percent of Oregon residents surveyed supported the harvest of old growth, 75 percent of Oregon and Washington residents surveyed in 2001 believed that old growth should be protected from logging on national forests, with slightly more support for this position in urban than in rural counties.

- Surveys in 1994, 1996, 1998, and 2000 consistently found that respondents believed the wood products industry was important to Oregon's economy. The more recent surveys, however, indicated that people believe the wood products industry would not be an important employer in the state in the future.

- A 1999 survey found that, of 15 forest management values, setting aside wilderness and clean drinking water were the top priorities for Oregonians surveyed. Economically healthy rural communities was sixth, and forest industry jobs was eleventh.

---

[2] 1 = not at all serious, 5 = very serious.

In 2001, Shindler et al. (2002) held focus groups in 14 communities in Oregon and Washington and surveyed a stratified random sample of households throughout Oregon and Washington to examine public understandings of the concept of "ecosystem health" on forest lands (482 households responded). They also investigated people's attitudes toward different forest management practices. The authors found that among the study participants from urban areas, 64 percent favored a balanced set of priorities for forest management, with 31 percent leaning strongly toward environmental protection, and 5 percent leaning toward economic management priorities. Of the rural residents surveyed, 69 percent favored a balanced approach, 18 percent favored environmental protection, and 14 percent favored economic management priorities. The findings of their study are almost identical to the findings of a similar study conducted 10 years earlier (Shindler et al. 1993, summarized above). When examining their findings based on residence, they found that rural residents were equally divided in terms of supporting environmental (30 percent) versus economic (32 percent) priorities, whereas urban residents showed a strong preference for environmental (45 percent) over economic (15 percent) priorities.

Two of five social criteria included in the study were considered by a majority of respondents to be important indicators of forest health: opportunities for recreation (70 percent) and stable rural communities (55 percent). Although a majority also considered regular economic returns by logging to be part of a healthy forest (46 percent, versus 31 percent who didn't), significantly more rural than urban respondents felt this way. In contrast, closing public access roads (53 percent versus 22 percent) and lack of human intervention (49 percent versus 26 percent) were not considered by most respondents to be indicators associated with forest health. Most people surveyed (87 percent) believed that active forest management over the long term was needed to maintain forest health.

The Heritage Forests Campaign sponsored a telephone poll by state to survey public opinion about national forest management when the Forest Service Roadless Area Conservation Rule was under development. From 800 registered voters surveyed in 2000 in California, they found that 58 percent opposed any development on national forest lands (mining, logging), and 34 percent favored these activities (HFC 2000). A similar poll conducted in 2000 among Oregon residents found that 45 percent opposed any development on national forest lands, and 51 percent favored development. Among Washington residents, 49 percent opposed allowing development-related activities on national forest lands, and 43 percent favored them (HFC 2000).

A telephone survey of randomly selected residents of Oregon, Washington, and northern California counties was administered by the Forest Service as part of a national survey of values, objectives, beliefs, and attitudes about forests and rangelands held by the American public (the VOBA survey) (Shields et al. 2002). The survey is national by design. The number of people included from Pacific Northwest counties was 433, but fewer than 100 of them were asked to respond to each question. The survey was conducted during 1998–99.

The forest management objectives that Pacific Northwest residents surveyed generally agreed were highly important (where 1 = not at all important and 5 = very important) were conserving and protecting forests and grasslands that are the source of water resources (4.63), informing the public about recreation concerns on forests and grasslands (4.49), protecting ecosystems and wildlife habitats (4.47), preserving people's ability to have a wilderness experience (4.21), and developing volunteer programs to improve forests and grasslands (4.43) (Shields et al. 2002). Their views about how well the Forest Service is managing for these objectives were only somewhat favorable (averaging 3.68 on a scale of 1 [poor] to 5 [well]). Management objectives that were not important to the majority of respondents were those related to developed recreation: expanding commercial recreation on forests and grasslands (2.77), expanding access for motorized off-highway vehicles (2.1), developing and maintaining trail systems across public and private lands for motorized vehicles (2.51), developing new paved roads on forests and grasslands (2.22), and making the permitting process for commercial recreational use and resource extraction easier (2.58). Providing forest resources to support communities that depend on timber harvesting, grazing, and mining was of moderate importance (3.58).

Opinions on how well the Forest Service is fulfilling this objective were essentially neutral (3.11).

As to respondents' individual values, people somewhat disagreed with statements suggesting that more trees should be actively harvested to meet the needs of a larger human population (2.2), that the most important role for public lands is to provide jobs and income for local people (2.71), and that the primary use of forests should be to produce products people can use (2.58).[3] Only slight agreement was found among respondents that public land managers are doing an adequate job of protecting natural resources from being overused (3.25).

Summary—

The most recent research from the Pacific Northwest on public attitudes, beliefs, and values about forest management indicates that people support a balanced set of priorities that includes both environmental and economic objectives. Environmental concerns predominate, however, especially among urban residents. Support for timber production appears to revolve around concern for rural communities, the lack of family-wage jobs available there, and the belief that healthy communities are important for forest health. Active forest management is generally believed to be necessary to maintain forest health. Most people asked did not favor harvesting old growth, however. Opinion is divided over whether federal forest managers are doing an adequate job of managing public forest lands sustainably.

Discussion and Conclusions

The forest management paradigm that prevailed in the Pacific Northwest following World War II emphasized high timber production by using techniques such as clearcutting, removal of logs and snags, slash burning, thinning, and planting single-species stands on harvested areas (FEMAT 1993: II-2-3). The agencies assumed that forests managed in this way could be harvested on a sustained-yield basis at 40- to 80-year intervals without negatively affecting other resources such as water quality, fish, soils, and wildlife. Studies conducted in the 1970s and 1980s made it apparent

---

[3] 1 = strongly disagree, 5 = strongly agree.

that this approach to forest management was not going to adequately protect the biodiversity of late-successional forests and associated aquatic ecosystems (FEMAT 1993: II-2-3). The forest management paradigm embraced in the 1990s under the Plan focuses on ecosystem management objectives that aim to sustain the underlying ecological processes of the forest (Johnson et al. 1993). Agencies are now placing more emphasis on managing for forest restoration, recreation, and other noncommodity values.

Was this paradigm shift supported by public attitudes, beliefs, and values regarding forest management in the Pacific Northwest, and do members of the public still support this management approach today? This literature review and synthesis suggest that the answer to both questions is "yes." Between 1990 and 2002 there has been surprisingly little change in Pacific Northwest residents' views of how Pacific Northwest forests should be managed. Throughout this period, research findings indicate that people support forest management to provide a broad set of multiple uses and both economic and environmental benefits. Nevertheless, there has consistently been a pro-environment leaning, with the majority favoring environmental over economic management objectives when asked to make a choice between them. Continued support for timber production from federal forests has likely been tied to a belief that the wood products industry is important to the regional economy, and to concern for the health of rural communities. Whereas place of residence was not found to be a significant factor influencing people's attitudes, beliefs, and values about forest management prior to the Northwest Forest Plan, recent studies find that urban residents tend to be pro-environment, with rural residents having more evenly split views on forest management issues.

Throughout the study period, the belief that active forest management improves forest health has predominated. However, clearcutting has consistently been unpopular, and the majority have favored old-growth protection. New forestry techniques that are not intensive are more socially acceptable.

Have federal land managers been doing a good job of protecting the forest values and environmental qualities people care about under the Plan? The research reviewed here does not provide extensive evidence for answering this question. The evidence that does exist suggests that opinion is fairly evenly divided. Some people have favorable views of the job forest managers are doing, and others believe that forest managers need to improve their performance. This question is addressed from the perspective of forest-based communities in the next chapter.

Acknowledgments

I am grateful to Julie Schaefers for helping to compile and summarize the literature for this chapter.

References

Clark, R.N.; Philpot, C.W.; Stankey, G.H. 1999. Overarching assumptions underlying the Northwest Forest Plan: imbedded implications for research at the PNW Research Station. Seattle, WA: U.S. Department of Agriculture, Forest Service, Pacific Northwest Research Station. 46 p.

Davis, Hibbitts, and McCaig, Inc. 2001a. A forestry program for Oregon: Oregonians discuss their opinions on forest management and sustainability—a quantitative research project. 71 p. On file with: Davis, Hibbits, and McCaig, Inc., 1100 NW Glisan, Suite 300-B, Portland, OR 97209.

Davis, Hibbitts, and McCaig, Inc. 2001b. A forestry program for Oregon: public opinion about forests and forest management in Oregon. A literature review. 34 p. On file with: Davis, Hibbits, and McCaig, Inc., 1100 NW Glisan, Suite 300-B, Portland, OR 97209.

Donoghue, E.M. 2003. Social values and compatible forest management. In: Monserud, R.A.; Haynes, R.W.; Johnson, A.C., eds. Compatible forest management. Dordrecht, The Netherlands: Kluwer Academic Publishers: 323–344. Chapter 15.

Forest Ecosystem Management Assessment Team [FEMAT]. 1993. Forest ecosystem management: an ecological, economic, and social assessment. Portland, OR: U.S. Department of the Interior [and others]. [Irregular pagination].

Fortmann, L.; Kusel, J. 1990. New voices, old beliefs: forest environmentalism among new and long-standing rural residents. Rural Sociology. 55(2): 214–232.

Hansis, R. 1995. The social acceptability of clearcutting in the Pacific Northwest. Human Organization. 54(1): 95–101.

Heritage Forests Campaign [HFC]. 2000. Public opinion poll on public attitudes and opinions toward land use issues in national forests. Oregon survey, California survey, Washington survey. http://www.ourforests.org/info/poll2000/. (May 3, 2000).

Johnson, K.N.; Crim, S.; Barber, K.; Howell, M.; Cadwell, C. 1993. Sustainable harvest levels and short-term timber sale options considered in the report of the Forest Ecosystem Management Assessment Team: methods, results and interpretations. Portland, OR: U.S. Department of Agriculture, Forest Service, Pacific Northwest Region. 66 p.

Proctor, J.D. 1998. Environmental values and popular conflict over environmental management: a comparative analysis of public comments on the Clinton forest plan. Environmental Management. 22(3): 347–358.

Ribe, R.G. 2002. Views of old forestry and new among reference groups in the Pacific Northwest. Western Journal of Applied Forestry. 17(4): 173–182.

Shields, D.J.; Martin, I.M.; Martin, W.E.; Haefele, M.A. 2002. Survey results of the American public's values, objectives, beliefs, and attitudes regarding the forest and grasslands: a technical document supporting the 2000 USDA Forest Service RPA assessment. Gen. Tech. Rep. RMRS-GTR-95. Fort Collins, CO: U.S. Department of Agriculture, Forest Service, Rocky Mountain Research Station. 111 p.

Shindler, B.; List, P.; Steel, B.S. 1993. Managing federal forests: public attitudes in Oregon and nationwide. Journal of Forestry. 91: 36–42.

Shindler, B.; Wilton, J.; Wright, A. 2002. A social assessment of ecosystem health: public perspectives on Pacific Northwest forests. Corvallis, OR: Oregon State University, Department of Forest Resources. 110 p.

Stankey, G.H.; Clark, R.N. 1992. Social aspects of new perspectives in forestry: a problem analysis. Milford, PA: Grey Towers Press. 33 p.

Steel, B.S.; List, P.; Shindler, B. 1994. Conflicting values about federal forests: a comparison of national and Oregon publics. Society and Natural Resources. 7: 137–153.

U.S. Department of Agriculture, Forest Service; U.S. Department of the Interior, Bureau of Land Management [USDA and UDSI]. 1994a. Final supplemental environmental impact statement on management of habitat for late-successional and old-growth forest related species within the range of the northern spotted owl. Vol. 2—appendices. [Place of publication unknown]. [Irregular pagination].

U.S. Department of Agriculture, Forest Service; U.S. Department of the Interior, Bureau of Land Management [USDA and USDI]. 1994b. Record of decision for amendments to Forest Service and Bureau of Land Management planning documents within the range of the northern spotted owl. [Place of publication unknown]. 74 p. [plus attachment A: standards and guidelines].

Chapter 2: Local Perceptions of Forest Protection and Issues and Concerns Regarding Forest Management

Susan Charnley and Ellen M. Donoghue

Introduction

People's perceptions of the effectiveness of agency management policies can influence their behavior and their attitudes toward the agencies. Although public perceptions may not always be "accurate" from the scientific standpoint, they matter, because these perceptions can drive appeals and lawsuits that prevent agencies from achieving their management objectives—regardless of what the science says. And if members of the public believe that agency management policies are ineffective at maintaining sustainable forest ecosystems, they may be critical and distrustful of the agencies, which can lead to a breakdown in relations. Socioeconomic monitoring can help managers become aware of these perceptions and complements biophysical monitoring related to the goal of forest protection.

The monitoring team interviewed community members from 12 case-study communities and agency employees from 4 case-study forests and documented their perceptions of how well the Plan had protected forest values and environmental qualities associated with older forests and aquatic ecosystems on federal forest lands. The results of these interviews are contained in chapter 2. Chapter 2 also documents community members' issues and concerns relating to forest management under the Plan

Monitoring Questions

1. From the public perspective, how well has federal forest management under the Northwest Forest Plan (the Plan) provided for forest values and environmental qualities associated with late-successional, old-growth, and aquatic ecosystems?

2. What issues and concerns related to federal forest management under the Plan are prevalent in local communities?

Expectations

A system of terrestrial and aquatic reserves established by the Plan would protect late-successional and old-growth forest (older forest) ecosystems inside of late-successional reserves, and the health of aquatic systems and the species that depend on them in riparian reserves and key watersheds (USDA and USDI 1994: 6-7). Late-successional reserves together with other Plan land use allocations and standards and guidelines would maintain a functional older forest ecosystem. Riparian reserves would help maintain and restore riparian structures and functions, benefit fish and nonfish species dependent on riparian ecosystems, and contribute to habitat conservation for terrestrial organisms.

Methods

The monitoring team found no studies that explicitly examined public views of how well the Plan has achieved the goal of forest protection. We conducted interviews with a total of 223 community members and 82 agency employees from four case-study areas (the Olympic, Mount Hood, and Klamath National Forests, and BLM Coos Bay District; and three local communities around each of these federal forests. See appendix). We asked them the following questions:

1: What are the two to three issues that community residents are currently most interested in or concerned about with regard to the management of forest x?

2: Have these been the main issues of interest/concern for the last decade? If not, how have the issues been shifting over the last decade, and why?

3: Do you (and the community you represent) think that Forest x has been doing a good job of managing for those forest uses, values, and environmental qualities that you care most about? Why or why not?

4: How could it do a better job of providing for the uses, values, and environmental qualities the community cares most about?

5: What progress has been made on meeting the Plan goal to help protect nontimber values and environmental qualities associated with the forest?

6:   An overarching goal of the Plan was to balance the need for forest protection with the need to provide a steady and sustainable supply of timber and non-timber resources to benefit rural communities and economies. Do you believe Forest/District x has been successful in achieving this goal? Why or why not? Examples?

The results of these interviews are summarized in this chapter, with a focus on the key findings common to all case-study areas.[1]

Results

Local Perceptions of Forest Protection

The case-study results point to some common themes about how well interviewees believe federal forest management under the Plan has achieved the goal of forest protection. The greatest successes were reported for aquatic ecosystems. Interviewees from the Olympic, Klamath, and Coos Bay areas commented that decreases in logging, road decommissioning, the provisions of the aquatic conservation strategy, the riparian reserve system, and the emphasis placed on watershed management and restoration under the Plan had protected and improved water quality.

Several interviewees commented that it would take a long time to see the benefits of the Plan for fish and wildlife populations, and reserved judgment on this topic. Several forest employees interviewed believed that survey and manage species requirements had led to a much better

---

[1] The information in this chapter is a summary of interview results discussed in more detail in the following

Buttolph et al. (in press).

McLain et al. (in press).

Charnley, S.; Dillingham, C.; Stuart, C.; Moseley, C.; Donoghue, E.M. Manuscript in preparation. Northwest Forest Plan—the first 10 years (1994–2003): socioeconomic monitoring of Klamath National Forest and three local communities. On file with: S. Charnley, Forestry Sciences Laboratory, 620 SW Main, Suite 400, Portland, OR 97205.

Kay, W.; Donoghue, E.M.; Charnley, S.; Moseley, C. Manuscript in preparation. Northwest Forest Plan—the first 10 years (1994–2003): socioeconomic monitoring of Mount Hood National Forest and three local communities. On file with: S. Charnley, Forestry Sciences Laboratory, 620 SW Main, Suite 400, Portland, OR 97205.

understanding of older-forest-associated species, their distribution and habitat requirements, and how to manage for them. Some community residents were concerned about the effects that reduced silvicultural activity would have on habitat for wildlife species—especially big game—that prefer early seral-stage forest and habitat mosaics. Some community residents interviewed around the Olympic and Klamath National Forests and the Coos Bay Bureau of Land Management (BLM) District believed local fish populations had increased, and attributed the increase to the Plan. Some interviewees believed that the Plan emphasized managing forests for the benefit of individual species instead of taking an ecosystem management approach that had the whole forest and its health in mind. On the other hand, several agency employees noted that the Plan had led to a more integrated approach to forest management. People were working across program areas and trying to manage forests in a more holistic way.

Community interviewees' views of the Plan's success at protecting forest habitat were not as positive, with most of them noting some undesirable results. There were interviewees from all four case-study areas who believed that pre-Plan timber-harvest rates were unsustainable and environmentally destructive, and were glad the Plan had brought an end to those practices—a substantial contribution to forest protection. It also brought a virtual halt to clearcutting practices on federal forest lands, which many interviewees approved. Nevertheless, some believed the Plan had not done enough to protect old growth because some older forest habitat was included in matrix lands and subject to logging pressure (not an issue on the Olympic National Forest). They attributed this problem to shortcomings in the original design of the Plan.

The Plan also brought new constraints that many interviewees believed had undermined forest protection goals. A widespread perception among interviewees was that silvicultural activity was needed to promote forest health. Specifically, thinning was seen as being necessary for reducing the risk of fire and disease, which threatened older forest habitat. Thinning was also seen as a strategy for expediting development of older forest habitat. Interviewees from all four case-study areas viewed federal forests as being overly dense because of past fire suppression practices and because of regenerating clearcuts and planted stands that were managed for timber before the Plan but had not been harvested or adequately thinned under the Plan. Thus, many interviewees believed that overall forest health had deteriorated because of the lack of active harvesting—especially thinning. And some believed this condition meant forests with little or no silvicultural treatments posed an imminent risk of fire danger, threatening both communities and older forest habitat.

Issues and Concerns in Relation to Forest Management

Many of the community members interviewed were unfamiliar with the specific components, forest management guidelines, and requirements of the Plan, and were unable to comment on it directly (although some were well informed about the Plan and its components). All, however, expressed issues and concerns regarding the management of nearby federal forests which were, at least in part, linked to Plan implementation. These indicate some of the ways in which the Plan has affected local communities.

The monitoring team found many parallels between the issues and concerns raised by community interviewees from the four case-study areas, although certain issues were more prevalent around some case forests than others. These centered on five topics: timber harvest, forest health and fire risk, forest-based jobs, recreation, and forest access and roads. A number of other issues arose that are not reported here because they were more specific to individual forests (such as noxious weeds, tribal relations, special forest products, law enforcement, water).

Timber harvest—
Most community interviewees believed that timber harvest on federal forest lands was unlikely to return to pre-Plan levels, and many felt those levels were unsustainable or destructive. Nevertheless, debate continues over the amount, frequency, location, and methods of timber harvest, and the types of trees involved. Issues under debate included the appropriate levels of commercial thinning, whether

or not old-growth trees should be harvested, probable sale quantity (PSQ) levels, and whether there should be timber sales in areas of the forest that have high environmental values (such as key watersheds), or where excessive environmental damage could result (such as steep slopes).

Many community interviewees also expressed concern that forests and districts were not meeting average annual PSQ estimates and providing a reliable supply of timber sales. Without a reliable timber supply, many buyers had difficulty operating and maintaining their infrastructure, and many contractors found it hard to stay in business unless they could rely on timber from private lands. Many people acknowledged that the agencies were trying to meet PSQ estimates, but perceived that the agencies' hands were tied by excessive procedural requirements, appeals, and litigation.

Forest health and fire—
In chapter 1, we report that the majority of people surveyed in the Pacific Northwest believe that actively managing forests by using silvicultural treatments improves forest health. A widespread perception among interviewees from the four case-study areas was that low levels of timber harvest and density management under the Plan have increased fire risk, insects, and disease, undermining forest health.

Concerns over fire were much more prevalent around the drier, fire-prone Klamath National Forest and eastern portion of the Mount Hood National Forest, than around the moist, lower-risk Olympic National Forest and Coos Bay District. On the Klamath National Forest, low-intensity fires naturally recur every 8 to 12 years, and stand-replacing fires recur every 80 to 180 years (USDA FS 1994: 3–115). On the Olympic National Forest, very large fires are rare, with major fires occurring at approximately 200-year intervals in prehistoric times (USDA FS 1990: III-85). On the Coos Bay District, stand-replacement fires are estimated to occur every 130 to 150 years (USDI BLM 1994: 3-131-132). Nevertheless, neighboring forest landowners, and communities around all four forests, were concerned that fires starting on federal lands could spread to their lands and burn their forests and homes, resulting in economic damage. Interviewees also expressed concern about the potential impact of fire on scenic quality around their communities, and on recreation and tourism.

Some people were also concerned about the spread of insects and disease. Others were concerned that densely stocked forests were detrimental to large game and other wildlife. Some interviewees expressed the view that the Forest Service (FS) had abrogated its responsibility for stewardship of federal forest lands by undertaking so little silvicultural activity under the Plan. Others believed that past timber harvest practices were bad for the forest, but that a complete lack of harvest activity was worse. Added to these sentiments was a common frustration that trees—which could produce useful products for people and provide jobs—were being left in the forest to die and rot.

Forest-based jobs—

Interviewees' concern over the perceived lack of timber harvest was based in part on the fact that federal forests were no longer a source of wood products and jobs for most community members. The dominant concern among long-time residents of the forest-based communities studied was the lack of family-wage jobs in their communities. Many jobs that were available in the timber and other natural-resource-based industries during the 1970s and 1980s are no longer available. Often young people and families must leave their communities to find work, breaking intergenerational family ties, making it impossible to pass trades down through generations, and causing a way of life to die out. Many community members interviewed viewed the forest as a place to work, and they wanted to find new ways in which federal forests could provide local, family-wage jobs that would allow them to stay in their communities and maintain family ties. Increasing access to timber for small locally-based mill operators and small businesses producing value-added products was also desired. Many community interviewees commented that the forests were unhealthy and in need of thinning and "cleaning up," which could provide local jobs.

Several interviewees from the Klamath National Forest (where recreation and tourism are less developed than on the other case forests) viewed forest fires and floods as the main source of local, forest-based jobs. Local people had

been successful in obtaining some fire suppression jobs and contracts for flood damage repair. Fires also brought people into the community who supported local businesses. In their view, natural disasters were a mixed blessing.

In sum, many interviewees believed that the FS in particular was overly concerned with protecting forest resources and should do more to create jobs in local communities. Environmental group representatives interviewed also supported forest-based job creation, as long as it occurred in a way that did not threaten ecological sustainability and old-growth forest ecosystems.

Recreation—

Recreation and tourism development hold potential for creating forest-based jobs. Recreation was a controversial issue on the case-study forests, with debates over the appropriate types, levels, and location of different recreation activities. Recreation and tourism development was also a controversial issue in the case-study communities. Those who supported it were typically business owners who stood to benefit. They cited jobs and economic development as benefits associated with forest-based recreation and tourism. Those who did not support it were concerned about its environmental impacts and effects on quality of life in their communities and questioned whether it would bring family-wage jobs.

Some interviewees were concerned that the FS was not maintaining the forest recreation infrastructure (such as campgrounds and trails) and forest access (roads) needed to attract visitors and promote recreation and tourism development in their communities. Others—around the Mount Hood National Forest in particular—were concerned that the forest was not adequately managing for growing recreation demand. Most interviewees around the BLM Coos Bay District strongly approved of the improvements the district had made to its recreation infrastructure. Many wanted to see this trend continue, because they believed it would support recreation and tourism development locally.

Community residents often enjoy recreating on surrounding federal forest lands themselves, and some of their issues of concern pertained to forest access for recreation opportunities they enjoy.

Roads and access—

The issue of forest access is related to the issues of recreation and forest-based jobs. The BLM and FS system road miles have decreased since 1994, and fewer roads are being maintained to passenger car standards. Roads damaged by storms are not always repaired in a timely manner, and overall road repair and maintenance is declining, causing road closures. These factors reduce forest access for a wide range of uses, including recreation, special forest products gathering, hunting, and fishing. At the same time they increase opportunities for nonmotorized recreational experiences. Not only do roads provide forest access, they distribute use and impacts. The only case-study area where community residents did not express concern over roads and access was the Coos Bay District, where road closures have increased because of gating on private lands.

Some community interviewees were concerned that recreation and tourism development would be hampered by reduced forest access. Others believed that the large sums of money spent on road decommissioning should be spent on road maintenance, which they thought was less costly and created long-term jobs.

Conclusions

The information in this chapter comes from four case-study locations in the Plan area. We focused on common themes that emerged from the four local cases, and do not know if, and to what extent, the results reported here can be generalized to the Plan area as a whole. In the places where we conducted fieldwork, members of the public interviewed perceived that the Plan had had mixed results to date for forest protection. Their issues of concern relating to forest management were to some degree linked to those perceptions.

The most positive Plan effects were believed to be associated with the protection of aquatic ecosystems. Most interviewees did not distinguish Plan effects on older forests from those on forest ecosystems more generally. Although the Plan brought an end to earlier forest management practices that many considered ecologically destructive, most people interviewed did not believe federal forests were

currently healthy. Like many Pacific Northwest residents surveyed in other studies (see chapter 1), they believed silvicultural activity was necessary for keeping forests healthy and that not enough had occurred during the first decade of the Plan. This led to concerns about fire, insects, and disease, and frustration that needed forest work was not creating local jobs. Timber harvest, forest health, and jobs were among the biggest issues of concern to community interviewees. The others were recreation and forest access, also tied to the issue of jobs. Although interviewees overwhelmingly believed that the Plan had emphasized forest protection over community well-being, their comments reflect a perception that healthy forest ecosystems and healthy community economies can and should be linked, and that those links are currently weak.

References

Buttolph, L.P.; Kay, W.; Charnley, S.; Moseley, C.; Donoghue, E.M. [In press]. Northwest Forest Plan— the first 10 years (1994–2003): socioeconomic monitoring of Olympic National Forest and three local communities. Gen. Tech. Rep. Portland, OR: U.S. Department of Agriculture, Forest Service, Pacific Northwest Research Station.

McLain, R.J.; Tobe, L.; Charnley, S.; Moseley, C.; Donoghue, E.M. [In press]. Northwest Forest Plan— the first 10 years (1994–2003): socioeconomic monitoring of Coos Bay District and three local communities. Gen. Tech. Rep. Portland, OR: U.S. Department of Agriculture, Forest Service, Pacific Northwest Research Station.

U.S. Department of Agriculture, Forest Service [USDA FS]. 1990. Final environmental impact statement, land and resource management plan, Olympic National Forest. Olympia, WA: Olympic National Forest. [Irregular pagination].

U.S. Department of Agriculture, Forest Service [USDA FS]. 1994. Klamath National Forest land and resource management plan. Yreka, CA: Klamath National Forest. [Irregular pagination].

**U.S. Department of Agriculture, Forest Service;
U.S. Department of the Interior, Bureau of Land
Management [USDA and USDI]. 1994.** Record of
decision for amendments to Forest Service and Bureau
of Land Management planning documents within the
range of the northern spotted owl. [Place of publication
unknown]. 74 p. [plus attachment A: standards and
guidelines].

**U.S. Department of the Interior, Bureau of Land
Management [USDI BLM]. 1994.** Coos Bay District
proposed resource management plan final environmental
impact statement. Vol. 1. North Bend, OR. [Irregular
pagination].

Appendix: People Interviewed for This Study

Case-Study Communities

When conducting interviews in the case-study communities, we attempted to select people that represented a cross section of community leaders and stakeholder groups. We also targeted people who had been community members since the Plan was adopted (1994). We used the following categories to guide our selection:

Community leaders
Elected official
Civic group leader
School district/education leader
Historic preservation/cultural center leader
Economic development council leader
Business leader/store owner
Social service provider
Fire district leader
Health official
Religious leader
Watershed council representative
Large landowner
Planner

Stakeholder group representatives
Recreation/tourism
Environment
Timber industry
Special forest products
Fishing—commercial/recreational
County government
Agriculture/ranching
Minerals
Tribes
Low income/minority groups

It was not possible to interview someone from each of the categories in every community, and many interviewees represented several categories at once. Descriptions of the interviewees from each community follow, by case-study area.

Olympic National Forest and Local Communities

Olympic National Forest

Respondent's position
Engineering program representative (3)
Forestry program representative (4)
District ranger (2)
Economic development representative
Public service representative
Forest planning representative
Forest supervisor
Aquatics program representative
Ecosystems/natural resources program representative
Wildlife biology program representative
Fire and aviation program representative
Operations staff representative
Timber contracting representative
Botany/forest ecology program representative
Recreation program representative
Information specialist
Tribal relations representative
Computer/mapping specialist

Quilcene

Respondent's position	Quilcene resident
Former logging contractor	X
Former logging contractor, business owner	X
Logging contractor, logging contractors' association	X
Local businessperson, recent immigrant (2)	X
Firefighter	X
Pastor	X
School official	X
County planning official (3)	
County planning official	X
Environmental interest group member	
Social service provider	X
Social service provider	
Economic development agency official	
County health and human services official (2)	
Industrial timberland manager	

Quinault Indian Nation

Respondent's position	Taholah/Queets resident
Quinault Tribal Council member, tribe member (2)	X
Quinault Indian Nation employee—forestry (2)	
Quinault Indian Nation employee—forestry, tribe member	X
Quinault Indian Nation employee—cultural historian, tribe member	X
Quinault Indian Nation employee—natural resources	
Retired logger, fisher, tribal elder	X
Basket weaver, tribal elder	X
School official	
Quinault Indian Nation employee—environmental protection	
Former Quinault Indian Nation employee—environmental protection	
Quinault Indian Nation employee—economic development	
Quinault Indian Nation employee—tribal liaison, tribe member	X
Basket weaver, Quinault Indian Nation employee—cultural historian, tribe member	X
Fisher, tribe member	X
Fisher, tribal elder	X

Lake Quinault Area

Respondent's position	Lake Quinault area resident
Former Park Service employee, local tourism-based business owner	X
Elected county official	
Fire district representative	X
School official	X
Waitress, school board member	X
Owner of log truck company, pastor, member of community/economic development organization	X
President of local chapter of national recreation organization	
Local tourism-based business owner, school board member	X
Retired rancher	X
Shake mill owner	X
Contractor for ecosystem management work on the forest	X
Representative from regional economic development organization	
Store owner	X
Representative from a regional environmental organization	

Mount Hood National Forest and Local Communities

Mount Hood National Forest

Respondent's position

Forest recreation, planning, public affairs staff officer
Forest planner, forest hydrologist
Forest geologist
Range program manager
Forest Youth Conservation Corps host and senior volunteer coordinator
Forest volunteer program coordinator
Fire and aviation management program manager
Forest silviculturist
Forest supervisor
Zigzag District Ranger
Forest natural resources staff officer
Forest special forest products coordinator
Public affairs officer, rural community assistance coordinator
Forest engineer
Vegetation management specialist
District and forest recreation program managers (group interview) (5)
Clackamas River District Ranger

Upper Hood River Valley

Respondent's position	**Upper Hood River Valley resident**
Former logger	X
Volunteer fire department chief	X
Long-time orchardist (2)	X
Environmental activist	X
Former logger	X
Retired Forest Service employee, now hobby orchardist	X
Retired Forest Service employee	X
Former logger	X
Orchardist, owner private timberland	X
County commissioner, family long-time residents	X
Local store owner, family long-time residents	X
Small mill operator, family long-time residents	X
Recreation industry representative	X
Program manager migrant worker social services, family long-term migrant workers, now residents	X
Regional soil and watershed association, and watershed association representative	
Confederated Tribes of Warm Springs employee, aquatic restoration program, office in case-study site	
Regional recreation industry representative	

Villages of Mount Hood

Respondent's position	Villages resident
Tourism and recreation industry rep	X
Tourism and recreation industry rep	
Developer, community development activist	X
Real estate services	X
Business person/chamber of commerce member	X
Watershed activists (2)	X
Long-time resident, community development activist	X
Retiree, service organization representative	X
News media representative	X
Local business owner	X
Logging contractor	X
Pastor	X
Firefighter	X
Logging contractor	
County Economic Development official	
Environmental interest group member (2)	
Industrial timberland manager	
Public school teachers (3)	X
Community development activist, seasonal resident	X
Community development activist	X

Estacada

Respondent's position	Estacada resident
Former logging contractors (3)	X
Forest service employees (4)	X
Logging supply store owner	X
Local businessman, town councilman	X
Logging contractor	
Firefighter	X
Local employer/business owner	X
Community activist, recent inmigrant	X
City manager	X
Local employer/business	X
Wilderness outfitter	X
County Economic Development official	
Environmental interest group members (2)	
Wood products company employees (3)	
Former business owner, chamber of commerce member	
Pastor	X
Social service provider	X
School official	X
Industrial timberland manager	

Klamath National Forest and Local Communities

Klamath National Forest

Respondent's position
Forest landscape architect
Forest resource staff officer (fisheries, noxious weeds, earth sciences, timber, wildlife)
District Ranger, Scott/Salmon Ranger Districts
Deputy forest supervisor
Forest silviculturist
District resource staff (recreation, range, noxious weeds, archaeology, minerals)
District archaeologist
Forest timber management officer and contracting officer, Shasta Trinity National Forest
Forest earth science and fisheries program manager
Forest administrative staff officer (contracting, community assistance program, volunteer programs)
Forest environmental coordinator
District recreation, lands/minerals staff
Forest fire management staff officer
Forest assistant engineer
Wildlife biologist

Scott Valley

Respondent's position	Scott Valley resident
Reforestation nursery owner	X
Director, nonprofit natural resources consulting and training center	X
Local mayor	X
Natural resource management interest group member	
Former county supervisor	X
Rancher, rural conservation district member	X
County board of education member	
Superintendent of schools (retired)	X
Forester, tree farmer	
County supervisor	X
Wood products company manager (2)	
Wood products company employee/forester	
Wilderness outfitter, natural resource management consultant/contractor (2)	X
Shasta Tribe member, retired timber worker	X
Shasta Tribe member	X
County behavioral health specialist	X
State Department of Forestry acting unit chief	X
County economic development corporation director	
County natural resource specialist	X
Environmental interest group member	X
County planning director	X
U.S. Forest Service district ranger (retired)	X
Salmon River Restoration Council representative, contractor, Mid-Klamath Watershed Council board member	X

Butte Valley

Respondent's position	Butte Valley resident
County Supervisor, Klamath Provincial Advisory Committee member, Ore-Cal Resource Conservation and Development Director, rancher	X
Ore-Cal Resource Conservation and Development employee	
Butte Valley Saddle Co. owner, chamber of commerce president	
Dorris Lumber & Molding	X
Vintage Woodworks owner	X
Shasta Tribe member, local environmentalist	X
Shasta Tribe member, former timber faller	X
Whitsell Manufacturing, Inc. (lumber remanufacturing)	X
TC Ranch owners	X
Butte Valley Fire District Fire Chief	X
Butte Valley Health Center	
Butte Valley Unified School District Superintendent	X
Butte Valley school district employee	X
Mayor of Dorris	X

Mid-Klamath

Respondent's position	Mid-Klamath resident
Local business owner/leader, county school board member, contractor, ex-mill worker	X
Fishing outfitter/guide, local school board member	X
Director, Happy Camp Family Resource Center (provides social services), local school board member, tribal council member	X
Retired Happy Camp district ranger, health clinic board member	X
Rancher, retired Forest Service employee	X
Miner, logger	X
Director, Karuk Economic Development Organization; Karuk Tribe member; vice president, Happy Camp Chamber of Commerce; chairman, Happy Camp Action Committee	X
Mid-Klamath Watershed Council representative, Klamath Forest Alliance representative	
Local business owner	X
Regional forest manager, fruit growers	
Karuk tribal member, special forest products gatherer, basket maker	X
Logger	X
New 49ers recreational mining club representative	X
Forest contractor, ex-logger, local business owner	X
Outfitter-guide, owner, local river rafting company	X
President, Happy Camp Chamber of Commerce, local business owner, Resource Advisory Committee member	X
Treasurer, chamber of commerce	X
Chair, Karuk Tribe	X
Vice Chair, Karuk Tribe	X
Secretary, Karuk Tribe	X
Anthropologist	X
Klamath-Siskiyou Wildlands Group representative	X
Klamath-Siskiyou Wildlands Group representative	

BLM Coos Bay District and Local Communities

Coos Bay District

Respondent's position

District manager
Resource area manager—Umpqua Resource Area
Resource area manager—Myrtlewood Resource Area
Noxious weeds program coordinator
Timber sales administrator
Silviculturalist
Watershed analysis coordinator
Small sales administrator—Myrtlewood Resource Area
Small sales administrator—Umpqua Resource Area
Volunteer coordinator
Cultural resources program manager
Recreation specialist (2)
Fish biologist
Wildlife biologist
Fire program manager
District geologist
Watershed restoration coordinator
Public affairs officer
Road engineer—Umpqua Resource Area
Road engineer—Myrtlewood Resource Area
Interpretive specialist

Greater Coos Bay

Respondent's position	Greater Coos Bay resident
Chamber of commerce employee (tourism focus)	X
Consulting forester/small woodland owners association member	X
County commissioner	X
County commissioner/rancher	X
County forester	X
Health services agency employee	X
Large timber company manager	X
Large timber company manager	
Large timber company manager, former local politician	X
Local economic development agency employee (tourism and industrial development focus)	X
Nature reserve employee	X
Tribal forester	X
Tribal member/fish biologist	X
Watershed association employee	
Watershed restoration contractor/forest worker	X

Greater Myrtle Point

Respondent's position	Greater Myrtle Point resident
Brush shed operator	X
Business development specialist	
Environmental educator	X
Environmental group leader	
Farmer/environmental educator	X
Fisheries specialist with state educational agency	
Large timber company manager	
Mountain bike club member/carpenter	X
Municipal leader	X
Public works employee	X
Restoration contractor/forest worker	X
Retiree, fisheries volunteer, long-term resident	
Retiree, rockhound club member, newcomer	X
Small mill operator	X
Watershed association employee	

Greater Reedsport

Respondent's position	Greater Reedsport resident
Cultural heritage organization leader/environmental education focus	X
Economic development leader/sportsfishing and tourism focus (2)	X
Economic development/elk viewing area involvement	X
Forest products company employee	X
Former school district leader	X
Former wood products industry employee/small mill operator	X
Industrial manufacturing company employee	X
Local politician	X
Manager of municipality	X
Member volunteer fire department	X
Municipal planner	X
Owner of local media	X
Rancher/mill owner/watershed organization member	X
Small business owner (timber related)	X
Small business owner, elk viewing area involvement	X
Social services organization manager	X
Timber company manager	
Wood products industry worker	X